THE
Gratitude
Power
Workbook

Also by Nina Lesowitz and Mary Beth Sammons

Living Life as a Thank You
The Transformative Power of Daily Gratitude

The Courage Companion
How to Live Life with True Power

THE Gratitude Power Workbook

*Transform Fear into Courage,
Anger into Forgiveness,
Isolation into Belonging*

By Nina Lesowitz and Mary Beth Sammons

VIVA
EDITIONS

Published in the United States by Viva Editions, an imprint of Cleis Press Inc., 2246 Sixth Street, Berkeley CA 94710.

Printed in China.
Cover design: Scott Idleman/Blink
Cover photograph: Daniel Sambraus/Getty Images
Text design: Frank Wiedemann
First Edition.
10 9 8 7 6 5 4 3 2 1

ISBN: 978-1-57344-649-5

Library of Congress Cataloging-in-Publication Data

Lesowitz, Nina.
 The gratitude power workbook : transform fear into courage, anger into forgive-ness, isolation into belonging / by Nina Lesowitz and Mary Beth Sammons.
     p. cm.
  ISBN 978-1-57344-649-5 (hardback)
1. Gratitude. 2. Conduct of life. 3. Quality of life. I. Sammons, Mary Beth. II. Title.
 BF575.G68L467 2011
 179'.9--dc22
                            2010049401

Contents

LIVING LIFE AS A THANK-YOU

Are you tired of walking around with a hole in your heart? Do you need more inspiration? Studies show—and experts counsel—that gratitude is a key component of our own happiness. People who are grateful about events and experiences from the past, who celebrate the triumphs instead of focusing on the losses or disappointments, tend to be more satisfied in the present. In her popular book *The Secret*, Rhonda Byrne writes, "With all that I have read and all that I have experienced in my own life using *The Secret*, the power of gratitude stands above everything else. If you do only one thing with the knowledge of the book, use gratitude until it becomes your way of life."

The recent buzz surrounding the power of gratitude is overwhelmingly positive. Jeffrey Zaslow, a columnist for the *Wall Street*

Journal, recently wrote that there may be a positive by-product of the troubled economic times that followed the 2008 stock market dive: a decrease in the urge to complain. "People who still have jobs are finding reasons to be appreciative. It feels unseemly to complain about not getting a raise when your neighbor is unemployed," he wrote. "Homeowners are unhappy that home values have fallen, but it's a relief to avoid foreclosure."

Indeed, in these times of economic woe, gratitude is popping up everywhere. Turn on the TV. We listened as a career coach on *The Today Show* advised job seekers to put the words "Thank you" in their job search tool kits, declaring that the key to distinguishing oneself from the masses is to send a thank-you note. Click onto Facebook and check out the gratitude groups, where hundreds of people log on each day to give thanks for everything from the sun rising that morning to their neighborhood dog parks. Cathy, of Greenville, South Carolina, wrote, "I am grateful for a bark park to take my dog-children to, so I picked up extra poop and trash this morning." Mary from Philadelphia wrote, "I am so grateful for the beautiful snow outside."

Gratitude floats our boats and moves us to do all kinds of things inspired by joy. Gratitude can help us transform our fears into courage, our anger into forgiveness, our isolation into belonging and another's pain into healing. Saying "Thank you" every day will create feelings of love, compassion, and hope.

But the fact is, the art of living—for that is what we speak about when we speak of gratitude—isn't something that comes naturally to most people. Most of us need to work intentionally to increase the intensity, duration, and frequency of positive, grateful feelings—a daunting challenge indeed. But fear not, this workbook is here to help! Inside we have provided you with mindful meditations, hands-on exercises, profound practices, inspiring quotations, space for writing, thought-provoking questions, and even positive "power tools" that will help you build a more grateful life.

After the publication of *Living Life as a Thank You*, we were surprised and heartened by the strong and immediate response to the book. It seemed that by writing about how we turned our lives around with the power of gratitude, we touched upon a great need. We've received hundreds of notes and e-mails from readers who expressed a deep gratitude for the book and its profound, practical advice. In an effort to fill this need to live a more fulfilling life through the power of gratitude, we have put together this workbook to help readers with the practical side of living gratefully, offering a strategic plan for infusing our daily lives with gratitude.

You might want to think of this workbook as a tool kit for personal transformation. No matter where you are on your life's journey, you can open this workbook to find inspiration, ideas for easy change, and exercises that will help you cultivate a more grateful, or perhaps "greatful," life. The workbook—at times sobering and at times challenging—will lead you to do the inner work required to grow and transform as a person, giving you pause and cause to explore the depths of your being. The questions, exercises, and meditations have been "road tested" by us, and we can tell you they will open up your life and allow you to let gratitude in. These practices do require you to do some thinking and some changing, and the results are very much worth the effort. We have also designed this workbook in such a way that you can use it in a group; the group guide is at the end of the book.

We know what it can be like when "living" seems to be just another item on your to-do list, and you find yourself struggling to incorporate positive daily practices into your life. But by taking just five minutes a day with this workbook, engaging the practices, meditations, exercises, and questions offered here, you'll find yourself moving toward a happier and more fulfilling life.

Imagine living as if each day were a gift. Imagine that everywhere you went people smiled and said, "Thank you," and you in turn were filled with joy and gratitude from the moment you woke up until you hit the pillow at night, your mind still and calm. Just imagine, a world without grumbling, a world where everyone is happy and grateful for where and who they are. Well, this is just the world we all hope to inhabit, and with help from this workbook, we'll all be a few steps closer.

With great-fullness,
Nina and Mary Beth

One

THANK-YOU POWER:
Your Well-Being

*Don't be concerned about being disloyal to your pain
by being joyous.*

—PIR VILAYAT INAYAT KHAN

We are living in groundbreaking, defining times. And quite naturally, with such moments of change and uncertainty comes the tendency to question how we will navigate the unknown. But with the promise of the new on the horizon, this an ideal time to reevaluate your own life and the spirit with which you face these challenges and bumps in the road.

We have come to learn that of all the tools we use to overcome these bumps—depression, anxiety, negativity, and physical or emotional illness—gratitude is the most effective (and the easiest!) method. Just as if you are mastering the craft of writing, or learning as a student in school, you need to practice expressing gratitude for life.

Take a look through these pages and you will discover the healing power of gratitude, a power that will help you to transform your challenges into opportunities. Internet social networks and blogs are abuzz with the idea of gratitude as healer. Humanity is coming to recognize that it is impossible to be grateful *and* hateful (or angry, sad, or discouraged) at the same time.

Gratitude promotes healing, harmony, peace, and joy. It encourages forgiveness, patience, and goodwill. It is a path that opens the opportunity for you to act on the good in your life. Even science backs this up. Sonja Lyubomirsky, professor of psychology at the University of California, Riverside, recommends that you make gratitude a daily practice, and it will bring healing properties into your life.

According to Robert Emmons—professor of psychology at the University of California, Davis—practicing gratitude is like exercising. Use it, and you won't lose it, even when times are tough.

Both Lyubomirsky and Emmons agree: those who practice an attitude of gratitude have lower risks for many health disorders, including depression and high blood pressure.

Practicing gratitude in systematic ways changes people by changing their brains that are "wired for negativity, for noticing gaps and omissions," Emmons says. "When you express a feeling, you amplify it. When you express anger, you get angrier; when you express gratitude, you become more grateful."

Gratitude has even shown the power to heal those in the depths of addiction. Once down and out, author Alan Kaufman firmly avows, "Gratitude is my life raft." Despite his struggles with alcohol addiction, he knew to tightly clutch his gratitude raft during the rough seas of his life. "There is a Hassidic saying, 'You should be grateful for everything that happens to you, even your pain,'" explains Alan, suggesting that you cannot think your way into right action, only act your way into right thinking. He continues, "So even if you don't feel like performing an act of service, but do it anyway, at a certain point you'll feel gratitude."

While most people think you have to be grateful to begin with to perform an act of service, it's often the other way around. "If you act in a principled way, you'll go from self-pity to a love for humanity," Alan says. "Gratitude is a direct path to that love."

Gratitude Meditation: Love

As Alan Kaufman has so eloquently stated, living life with thankfulness can bring love into your life, making you altogether a more loving being. And who doesn't want love in their life? This loving kindness meditation should do just that.

Begin by sitting down and clearing your mind. Breathe deeply, in and out ten times. Picture all the people you love, one by one. Receive the warm sensation of love from them and allow it to enfold you in a veritable "blanket of love." Now, return this love, silently whispering, "I love you" to each one. End by saying the same to yourself. Hold this through the day.

Gratitude Exercise:

JUST WHAT THE DOCTOR ORDERED

Neuropsychiatrist David Amen, MD, believes that thoughts carry physical properties and that the properties of negative thoughts can be detrimental to your leading a healthy, happy life. To overturn these negative effects, he prescribes thinking more positively, maintaining that by doing so, you can change the way your brain works and in turn change your life for the better. With this in mind, write down ten negative thoughts that you've had in the past week, and think of a way to be grateful for each of them.

Examples:

I wish my brother would stop asking me for money.

I am grateful that I have the finances to support those I love in tough times.

1. ....

....

....

2. ....

....

....

3. ....

....

....

4. ....

....

....

5. ....

....

....

6. ....

....

....

7. ....

....

....

....

8.

9.

10.

Gratitude Practice:

WRITE YOUR LIFE

Throughout this book, you'll find space for keeping your own gratitude journal. At the end of each day, write five things from the day you feel grateful for: a smile from a stranger, a hug from your child, an unexpected compliment, a good meal, or a moment of laughter with a friend.

REST WELL

Go to bed with gratitude. Think about all you appreciate from the day that just passed, breathing deeply and relaxing as you do so.

GATHER THE GRATEFUL

Bring a group of friends together for a gratitude gathering and recount the things each of you is grateful for. Conclude with a celebratory potluck meal.

Let us be grateful to people who make us happy—they are the charming gardeners who make our souls blossom.

—MARCEL PROUST

WRITE YOUR LIFE

*Wake at dawn with a winged heart and
give thanks for another day of loving.*
—KAHLIL GIBRAN

Something opens our wings.
Something makes boredom and hurt
  disappear.
Someone fills the cup in front of us.
We taste only sacredness.

—RUMI

Expressing gratitude is a natural state of being and reminds us that we are all connected.

—VALERIE ELSTER

....

....

....

....

....

....

....

....

Happiness is not so much in having as sharing. We make a living by what we get, but we make a life by what we give.

—Norman MacEwan

MAKING HAY

Inspirational author Louise Hay healed herself from cancer through positive visualization. A true believer in the power of the positive, Louise forewent conventional Western medicine, eschewing her doctor's advice (not necessarily something we recommend) and instead decided to use the power of forgiveness to overcome her cancer. Louise contends that the weight of the anger and resentment that we harbor invariably will hold us down, and we must forgive or let go of these painful moments in order to fully heal. If forgiving those in her past enabled Louise to defeat cancer, surely it can help you with your own troubles. What are you able to let go of that's holding you back? Whom or what can you forgive to help unburden your soul?

Following are some affirmations from the indefatigable Louise herself:

> "I am ready to be healed. I am willing to forgive. All is well."

> "There is plenty for everyone, and we bless and prosper each other."

Gratitude Questions:

SEEKER, HEAL THYSELF

1. *What reservoirs of pain are you storing?*

....

....

....

....

....

....

....

2. *Do you know why you are holding onto them?*

....

....

....

....

....

....

....

....

3. *Do you know the difference between a "good grudge" and a "bad grudge"? Martha Beck recounts in her excellent book* Leaving the Saints *that forgiving her father for abuse and neglect allowed her to heal and achieve a true wholeness. A good grudge, she contends, can protect you from people who will mess up your life, like the flakey friend who has cancelled plans five times at the last minute, causing you stress and costing you your valuable time and money. Are you holding any good grudges? Bad ones?*

....

....

....

....

....

....

....

....

4. *What or whom should you forgive? List them here.*

Two

GRATEFUL FOR THE GOOD LIFE:
Turning Your Life Around

The winds of grace blow all the time. All we need to do is set our sails.

—SRI RAMAKRISHNA PARAMAHAMSA

There is an expression that says if you want to turn your life around, try thankfulness, because finding reasons to be grateful every day can be the key to living an abundant life.

We all know people who find beauty at every turn of the road. They are really and truly grateful for each and every encounter—the smile on a stranger's face, the kindness of the grocery store clerk. When you are around these people, it sets your vibrations higher; it makes you aware that you are responsible for attracting all those things that will make your life more complete.

Grateful people, you will discover, seem to be more resilient. They seem to have an easier time overcoming obstacles. Grateful people are more appreciative of others and, in being so, more willing to give back in gratitude. They realize how others have helped them, and they take nothing for granted.

Many persons look at grateful people and say they are lucky or blessed, or just fortunate. But in truth, grateful people simply understand that gratitude is a signature strength. They make a point to train their gratitude muscle every day, just as if it were their heart, or their mind, or their body on a treadmill.

The result: grateful people have a sense of wonder and look at the world through the eyes of astonishment and joy. By focusing on what they have and being grateful for it, they bypass feelings of neediness, anger, or greediness.

Texas entrepreneur Anthony Migyanka is a prime example an especially thankful person. "I use spoken gratitude in my daily life to produce much success and contentment," he says. "First of all, in my business, after I decide on a course of action, I say, 'Thank you,' for the results not yet obtained, for the future gratitude of today."

He laughs when he explains that he speaks clearly but "usually with no one around," rattling off his list of to-be-thankful-for future events. The checklist may include "Thank you" for a productive meeting, "Thank you" for letting my company find the right vendor, or "Thank you" for a job well done.

Giving thanks in his personal life is an especially profound daily practice for Anthony. "Using spoken gratitude frequently, daily, has really made a difference in my life," he says. "It has made me calmer, less fearful, and happier. After the spoken gratitude, it's like I can move on to the business at hand, and be present, as the saying goes, and not work with a divided mind on things."

When you realize that life flows through your attitudes and actions, you create a channel for the universe to move through you to connect with others. Your own attitude of gratitude is one of the important lessons and legacies parents can pass on to their children: If you are bound by gratitude and grace to speak of it, incorporate it into your connections with others.

Gratitude Meditation:

SAY IT, THINK IT, FEEL IT

Expressing your gratitude in every possible way will pave the path to a state of *Santosh*, the Hindu concept for contentment. In this hurly-burly world, how many people do you know who are satisfied? Again, we should all be grateful for all that we have, not strive and stress for materials and "things" that bring us only a momentary endorphin rush with little real contentment.

For this Santosh Session, get up and stand facing the sun. Hold up your arms in a sun salutation and say, "I am glad to be alive on this beautiful day. I feel grateful to have my health and the gift of life. For all that I have, I am grateful and content."

Gratitude Exercise:

APPRECIATION

We have seen this excellent exercise put into practice at work, family reunions, and dinner parties. It never fails to bring a group of people closer, and it brings out the best in anyone. It is especially effective among a group of fractious folk, and it calms roiling waters easily. Time your moment well; never at the beginning of a get-together. Whenever there is a lull would be best. Call everyone to attention and say you want to acknowledge your appreciation for the group. Do so with simple statements.

Examples:

> "What I appreciate about Matt is his humility; he is brilliant but never showy."

> "What I appreciate about Brian is his kindness and generosity. He helped me out when I was in a bad way. I will always be grateful to him for that."

Offer a positive appreciation for each person and encourage others to do the same. Talk about a "turnaround"—this can turn stormy skies blue in five minutes flat.

1. ....
....
....
....

2. ....
....
....
....

3. ....
....
....
....

4. ....
....
....
....

5.

6.

7.

8.

9.

10.

PASS IT ON!

Write a letter of gratitude to the people in your everyday life who make a difference—the mailman, a grocery clerk, or the greeter at the mall. Tell your friends about their places of business or their great service so their businesses can grow.

TEACH YOUR CHILDREN WELL

Sit down with your child and ask him or her to create a prayer of thankfulness. Provide a simple starting point: "Thank you for…" Then ask your child to draw a picture to go with the prayer.

PAY IT FORWARD

Select someone who needs a gesture of kindness. Perhaps think of something kind that someone once gave to you. With gratitude for what was given, reach out and give back. It can be a simple gesture, like sending a card, or calling someone who is sick and saying you care.

When we recognize the Divine Presence everywhere, then we know that it responds to us and that there is a Law of God, a Law of Love, forever giving of itself to us.

—ERNEST HOLMES

WRITE YOUR LIFE

Happiness cannot be traveled to, owned, earned, worn or consumed. Happiness is a spiritual experience of living every minute with love, grace, and gratitude.

—DENIS WAITLEY

If the only prayer you said in your whole life was "Thank you," that would suffice.

—Meister Eckhart

Gratefulness—the simple response of our heart to this life in all its fullness— goes beyond boundaries of creed, age, vocation, gender, and nation.

—J. ROBERT MOSKIN

....

....

....

....

....

....

....

....

GIVING THANKS, LET US COUNT THE WAYS

A globetrotting friend of mine told me that the first thing she would do before setting foot in another country was learn how to say, "Thank you," in the native language. "You'd be surprised at the delight others take in hearing a foreigner's tongue speak their own language," she said. "They were sometimes surprised, other times impressed, and sometimes they would have no idea what I was saying! But they were always grateful for my attempts."

Here's a list of the world's many ways to express your gratitude:

Arabic:	Shukran
Czech:	Děkuji
Danish:	Tak
Dutch:	Dank u
Estonian:	Tänan teid
Filipino:	Salamat
Finnish:	Kiitos
French:	Merci
Gaelic:	Go raibh maith agat
German:	Danke
Hungarian:	Köszönöm
Indonesian:	Terima kasih
Italian:	Grazie
Japanese:	Arigato
Latvian:	Paldies
Norwegian:	Takk
Polish:	Dziękuję
Portuguese:	Obrigado
Romanian:	Mulțumesc
Spanish:	Gracias
Swahili:	Asante
Swedish:	Tack
Vietnamese:	Cảm ơn bạn
Welsh:	Diolch yn fawr

Gratitude Questions:
DON'T JUST THINK IT, SAY IT!

1. *Do you vocalize your thanks? All the time? Could you more?*

....

....

....

....

....

....

....

....

2. *Who are the people in your life who set your "vibration to a higher level"?*

....

....

....

....

....

....

....

....

3. *How could you become a person who uplifts others?*

....

....

....

....

....

....

....

Three

GRATITUDE AS A SPIRITUAL PRACTICE

We all have angels guiding us. They look after us. They heal us, touch us, and comfort us with invisible warm hands. What will bring their help? Asking. Giving thanks.

—SOPHY BURNHAM

In all our lives, we experience mysterious happenings. Some call them coincidence, others synchronicity, and others God.

But when you look at the world through the lens of gratefulness and thanks for what is, life becomes an answered prayer. Grace steps in, and you develop a faith that hope is possible.

Grace and gratitude can be spiritual forces that propel you ahead. They guide you, and you must learn to call on the energy of this life force. Soon, you realize that you are never alone, and you can move out of your own way and make room for the blessings in your life to follow.

Gratitude can be used as a powerful spiritual tool in your life as well. Learn to begin your days praying for the gift of gratitude to see the blessings in your life. Then, go about your day being receptive and alert to these movements of grace and gratitude. The more you do this, the more a kind of magnetic force moves into place to draw blessings toward you.

Knowing how to spot the moments when you are moved to grow spiritually and emotionally is important to living life with a spirit of gift and gratitude, as is recognizing the deeper meanings when an everyday person shares what she has to offer.

Author Phil Cousineau talks about such a spiritual moment in his book, *The Way Things Are: Conversations with Huston Smith on the Spiritual Life*. This most gratifying moment took place when Cousineau joined Smith, a preeminent scholar of world religions, in Cape Town, South Africa, at the World Parliament of Religions in 1999. The two sat in on the signature speech by former South African president, Nelson Mandela, where, as Phil recollects, "Dame Fortune smiled on us, and we were able to sit only a few rows from the stage. In deference to Huston's hearing problem I tried repeating the opening words of Mandela's speech in his ear. But after a few failed attempts to pick up my whispers, Huston raised his hand, signaling me to stop, and whispered back, 'It is enough for me to be within Mr. Mandela's *darshan.*'"

"What struck me was the utter raptness of Huston's attention, the dignity of his bearing as he practiced the ancient Indian ritual of *darshan*, which means sitting quietly and humbly in the presence of someone whom you revere, growing simply from being there," says Phil.

Phil understands that the wisdom of people is not only made present through their words and actions, but also through their spirit, through their very being, and it is for this moment that Phil is forever grateful.

Gratitude Meditation: Acceptance

Spend some moments and think about your own life. In what areas are you challenged by an imperfection, a disability, a block, or something seemingly as small as a piece of sand? Instead of trying to throw it away, destroy it, curse it, label it, or deny it, try to accept and love it. It will be transformed like magic from your inner enemy to your inner guide; from your imperfection to your perfection; from your disability to your Jewel.

Breathe in three times. Imagine that you are breathing in your imperfections. Now breathe out three times. Imagine that you are breathing out your perfections. Between breaths, spend a few seconds imagining that your gratitude for everything that you are is ascending to the skies and surrounding the world like the oyster's shell surrounds the pearl. May all your challenges be transformed into pearls.

Gratitude Exercise:

PROMPT YOURSELF WITH PRAYER

Create gratitude prayer prompters. With these prompts, you'll be able to incorporate gratitude prayers into your life by using common sensory information from daily living as a trigger to remind you to be grateful for what is right in front of you. Each time you come across these visuals, remind yourself to halt your thoughts for a minute and say a prayer of intentional thanksgiving.

Examples:

> A fire truck or an ambulance: Say, "Thank you," for the men and women who are there to take care of the sick and hurting.
>
> A police car: Pray for those whose lives are in trouble and give thanks for those who serve, counsel, and protect.
>
> A school bus: Give thanks for children everywhere. Pray for your children and pray for the children worldwide who will never have the opportunities you have had.
>
> A church or spiritual place: Remember your blessings. Then pray for those in need or for those who don't have the grounding and blessings of faith.

Gratitude Exercise:

CRAFT GRATITUDE

Create your own prayer book. Cut out pictures from nature magazines of inspirational or spiritual scenes and paste them in a spiral notebook. Then add quotes and prayers to create your own inspirational prayer book. Leafing through it can remind you of what you are grateful for and remind you to give thanks in prayer.

....

....

....

....

....

....

....

....

....

....

DAILY AFFIRMATIONS

1. I am appreciative of all the "tough times" in my life as I have grown from them.

2. I am learning, everyday, how I can be a better person.

3. As I grow in gratitude, I want to give equally. I give through service.

4. Each day, I give thanks for the gift of life.

5. I am glad to have figured out that the people that I have the most problems with are the ones I can learn the most from.

6. I treasure my friends, family, and loved ones, and for that, each day is Thanksgiving.

7. I am becoming a more conscious and integrated person each day. It's not so easy, but I am fortunate to live in a society that encourages it.

8. I am blessed. May others be, as well.

9. We are here to love and to give. I shall love more, each and every day.

10. Every day is an opportunity. I will seize each day. *Carpe diem*!

Whoever you are—I have always de-
pended on the kindness of strangers.

—BLANCHE DUBOIS (IN *A STREETCAR*
NAMED DESIRE, BY TENNESSEE WILLIAMS)

WRITE YOUR LIFE

The most powerful moral influence is example.

—Huston Smith

....

....

....

....

....

....

....

....

....

A merry heart does good like a medi-cine.

—Proverbs 17:22

....

....

....

....

....

....

....

....

....

God is in the details.

—Ludwig Mies van der Rohe

....

....

....

....

....

....

....

....

....

....

Gratitude Power Tools:

KEEP YOUR SPIRITS UP!

Looking for ways to tap into the spiritual power of gratitude? Gahl Eden Sasson, a spiritual teacher and author of *Cosmic Navigator: Design Your Destiny with Astrology and Kabbalah*, shared with us his tools for committing to the spiritual awakening of the power of gratitude in your life.

Om Mani Padme Hum is an old Buddhist prayer designed to invoke compassion and unconditional love. It is a prayer you can call on to help you tap into your wellspring of gratitude.

In Tibet, this mantra is written on prayer wheels, which are then spun continuously. These prayer spheres resemble the ten spheres of the Tree of Life and work in a similar way.

The meaning of this prayer is very profound. It translates to "The Jewel is in the Lotus." The Lotus is a flower that grows in water (the symbol of compassion in Kabbalah as well as in Buddhism) out of the mud and dirt. From the darkest and most hidden places the perfect flower emerges.

The Jewel is the pearl. The story of the pearl is the story of the transformation of imperfections and disabilities into a wondrous jewel. The pearl is created when a piece of grit, dirt, or sand is caught in the oyster. The oyster, being another profound symbol of compassion, does not discard the piece of dirt nor does it throw it away as we humans do with our own garbage and dirt. The oyster caresses it with a white veil. Like a silent kiss, it embraces the dirt, investing in it love and kindness. Slowly, with patience, the piece of worthless dirt becomes a precious pearl.

The oyster teaches us that we need imperfection (the dirt) to create perfection (the pearl). We should treat our imperfections and disabilities the same way the oyster treats the grain of sand. It simply accepts it.

Kabbalah in Hebrew means "to accept." Kabbalah teaches us how to flow with God's work by accepting it. The oyster holds that same secret; it teaches us to accept our weaknesses and disabilities. We are perfect in our imperfections; that is the secret paradox of life. What makes us perfect is the ability to grow, and we can only grow if we are not yet perfect. As long as we have some imperfections, we are participating in God's creation.

That is the key of life and that is the Jewel in the Lotus. We often spend too much time in gratitude for what is going well in our life, but as God is One, the perfect and imperfect in you are also one. Spend some time focusing on showing your gratitude toward the imperfections that make you so perfect.

Gratitude Questions:

SAY A LITTLE PRAYER

Because spirituality infuses your life with stability and a sense of purpose, take the time now to reflect on those things your spirituality provides you with for which you are truly thankful, and then answer these questions:

1. *What feeds your soul? List as many things as you can.*

....

....

....

2. *Who, in your life, provides you with spiritual sustenance? Who do you in turn provide this with? How might you do more?*

....

....

3. *Can you offer more to the people in your life? Your family, coworkers, community?*

....

....

Four

PRACTICING GRATITUDE IN EVERYDAY LIFE

There are only two ways to live your life. One is as though nothing is a miracle. The other is as though everything is a miracle.

—ALBERT EINSTEIN

Have you ever made a wish for happiness when blowing out your birthday cake candles? Instead of making a wish for what you don't have, or what you want, stop and think about what you do have and what you are grateful for. You'll find yourself appreciating your home, even though it needs work; your significant other, even though he or she is lacking in any number of qualities; and your day-to-day life, despite its ups and downs.

We all have moments in our lives that are cause for big celebrations and thank-yous—birthdays, graduations, holidays, a new baby, or a job promotion. It is easy to pull out the champagne, light the candles on the cake, and go all out in celebration. But it is embracing the joyful simplicities of every day and discovering their simple delights that are the essence of life. You need to find joy, to be thankful for the everyday moments that bring you comfort and well-being.

All it takes is a shift in your thinking, a mindfulness to focus on what makes you glad to be alive. So, the next time you're driving down the street with your mind full of tasks, take a look at the people strolling along the sidewalks. Notice the ones who have smiles on their faces. Those are the folks who are enjoying their walk; they're appreciating the scenery. Sometimes there is no more profound advice than "Stop and smell the roses."

Gratitude Exercise:

SCENTS AND SENSIBILITY

Think about your favorite smells and how they affect you. Bergamot's delightfully citrus scent can add some zest and energy to your step. Lavender can be particularly calming and restorative. The sweet fragrance of jasmine flowers always stops me in my tracks, and rosemary is known for its ability to improve memory. When you're feeling down or ungrateful, seek out these delightful scents. They will lift your spirits and give you a moment, as you breathe in their fragrance, to reflect on the simple, yet wonderful things all around you for which you can be grateful.

Write down your seven favorite smells. Put as many different flowers or herbs on your list as you can.

1. ....

2. ....

3. ....

4. ....

5. ....

6. ....

7. ....

MINDFULNESS MOMENTS

These simple moments, when life shows us its blessings, can be empowering ones. And just as slowing down and enjoying the aromas of life can help to heal our spirits and fill our gratitude wells, so too can listening—simply to the sounds of nature around you, or to what your loved ones are saying. Doing so allows you to give a gift of love, free of judgment or expectation.

When you acknowledge what you've learned from others, it helps you begin to appreciate the abundance in your life. Sometimes, it also helps you to tap into the positive qualities that you embody. Gratitude attracts more gratitude and opens the gates of tenderness. Be the first to reach out in the midst of fear and uncertainty to listen, care, and be present.

Creating a sacred space where you can celebrate your thankfulness is not something you often think of doing. But thanks to Lindsey Rodarmer, you learn that it is necessary to carve out time, energy, and intention to experience and bring forth your feelings of gratitude for what you are and what you have in your life.

In this tough economy, Lindsey and her husband Ryan, to go along with their busy, stressful publishing jobs, also moonlight to pay the bills and try to get ahead. She says that these days, they "often feel like there is no light at the end of the tunnel in this economy." But, she adds, they hear about friends who have lost their jobs and are struggling to provide for themselves and their small children. "These people would do anything to find some kind of work," says Lindsey. "This past weekend, we even heard about a man who had to move from Michigan to Wyoming for work, leaving his wife and twin daughters behind. They can't even see each other because it's too costly for him to travel back and forth."

The couple has learned from stories like these that they must remain grateful for what it is they do have. In order to keep that deep awareness at the front of her mind all day long, Lindsey has created a "gratitude list" that hangs in her office. The list includes the top ten things for which she is grateful. "Whenever I get down at work, I look at this and remind myself why I am here and why I am so lucky," she says.

Here is Lindsey's list:

1. Braiden is healthy and happy. [Braiden is Lindsey's stepson.]

2. Our health, especially Ryan's health. [Ryan recently recovered from a dangerous heart infection.]

3. Marrying for true love, not money, and knowing deep down that we would be happy together, even if we had to give up everything we owned and live in poverty.

4. A safe place to live and food to eat.

5. Our family and friends—so many wonderful people that we hang out with not just because we have to, but we want to.

6. Our jobs (all four of them!).

7. Having the opportunity to teach and shape young minds, and continue learning right along with them. [Lindsey teaches adjunct college courses.]

8. Our dog, who is forever happy to see us and never complains.

9. We get to go on vacation this summer as a family— remember to save money all year for that one glorious week—pay cash and have no debt from this vacation.

10. Sharing faith, hope, and trust, that things are out of control anyway, so why not make the best of what we can and live each day as positively as possible?

NOW MAKE YOUR OWN TOP TEN LIST.

1. ....
....
....

2. ....
....
....

3. ....
....
....

4. ....
....
....

5. ....
....
....

6.

7.

8.

9.

10.

Gratitude Meditation:

WALKING

Try a walking mediation the next chance you get. Whether it is a walk around the block, in a park, or on the beach, just begin walking and empty your mind of tasks, troubles, and worries and *just be*. Observe your surroundings with fresh eyes and enjoy the beauty around you, even it is a flower blooming through a crack in the sidewalk.

Gratitude Practice:

STATES OF GRACE

Using any of the gratitude practices throughout this book, shift into a state of gratitude. Then make a wish, and see if it comes true!

UNCONDITIONAL LOVE LESSONS

If you have a pet, take a few moments to list the blessings your beloved animal brings to your life. Perhaps your cat keeps your toes warm at night, or your dog gets you outside every day for fresh air and exercise. Give thanks for the unconditional love of your pet.

EVERYDAY ABUNDANCE

Stop for a moment and be thankful for the giver behind the gift. Make a list of the people in your life who made you happy today. It could be anyone—the clerk at the grocery store who knows you and took the extra time to ask how you and your loved ones were doing, the neighbor who shoveled your sidewalk, or the friend who called unexpectedly just to say she cared. Practicing gratitude is about being thankful for all the blessings in your life—the abundance found in each and every day.

Light a Virtual Candle

Light a candle with the intention of saying thanks for what you are grateful for in your life. If you don't have a candle handy, or are not in a place where that is practical, go to www.gratefulness.org/candles/enter.cfm?l=eng and you can light a candle in solidarity with others who have found their way to Brother David Steindl-Rast's gratefulness community. Gratefulness.org is a nonprofit organization dedicated to gratefulness as a universal principle that serves as the core inspiration for personal growth, cross-cultural understanding, interfaith dialogue, intergenerational respect, and ecological sustainability.

Gratefulness is the key to a happy life that we hold in our hands, because if we are not grateful, then no matter how much we have we will not be happy—because we will always want to have something else or something more.

—BROTHER DAVID STEINDL-RAST

WRITE YOUR LIFE

....

....

....

....

....

....

....

Your diamonds are not in far distant mountains or in yonder seas; they are in your own backyard, if you but dig for them.

—RUSSELL H. CONWELL

Who does not thank for little will not thank for much.

—Estonian proverb

....

....

....

....

....

....

....

....

....

I merely took the energy it takes to pout and wrote some blues.

—DUKE ELLINGTON

Gratitude Power Tools:

HAPPY FOR THE LITTLE THINGS IN LIFE

We talk a lot about being grateful for what you have received, but what is there that you can give? How can you go through your daily life giving cause for gratitude in others—family, friends, coworkers, strangers?

1. **Thoughtfulness.** You know your coworker works really hard and can come in a bit bedraggled from an arduous week. Why not walk up to her and say, "Good Morning!" handing her a vitamin-rich protein Smoothie?

2. **Helping Hand.** Your new neighbor is an elderly widow. Every Sunday night, when you go to take out your own garbage and recycling, knock on her door and offer to take hers out, too. You might even be invited in for tea and cookies, as I was!

3. **Lending Ear.** Listening is one of the greatest gifts you can give anyone. As humans we all want to be heard. So, start by listening a little more each day. Listen to your children, your spouse, your friends, even the Chatty Cathy in the office. You, in turn, will be repaid by being listened to with far more attention and care.

4. **Kindness.** Get acquainted with the power of simple goodness, as illustrated by the Hawaiian island tradition of "Living Aloha," which is the Native Islanders' way of daily living— simple acts of goodness every day. When at the grocery store, return the cart, help the elderly man struggling with his bags. Open doors for people; say, "Hello," with a smile. Every day and in every way choose to take the high road in your travels. The view is much more beautiful up top!

Gratitude Questions:

LIVE A LITTLE

1. *Other than birthdays, anniversaries, and promotions, what have you celebrated of late?*

....

....

....

....

....

....

2. *Life is made up of both little things and big. It is the little moments pieced together that make up a life. What little moments can you celebrate?*

....

....

....

....

....

....

3. *How can you provide more positive little moments for yourself? For loved ones? For strangers?*

....

....

....

....

....

....

....

....

....

....

Five

STAYING THANKFUL IN DIFFICULT TIMES

No one wants to endure heartache or suffering. None of us would voluntarily choose to lose our jobs, see our family members struck down by illness, or have a cherished relationship end. But it is often after these times of difficulty, heartache, and anguish that blessings come.

Many believe that strength comes only through struggle. It is a common refrain that what doesn't kill us makes us stronger. Ironically, many of us find we become more compassionate, more caring, and better people after we have moved through difficulties or periods of trauma.

We are inspired by the creative ways people facing difficult times have dug beneath the surface to uncover what they are grateful for.

They help us find ways to articulate our thankfulness and remind us that no matter what challenges we face in life, rainbows follow clouds and rain.

Sometimes it is in your darkest moments that you need to trust that a power greater than you will help you to move out of your despair. How many times have you cried out in anguish, "God, please help me?," and then realized that no matter what is taken away, no matter what hurricane rips through your life, you will survive, and you are grateful for everything you have had so far.

When adversity hits your life, sometimes you feel like you have been thrown into a tornado, spun around, shaken up, and spit back out into the world, stripped of what was there before, confused, lost, and afraid of what lies ahead.

Troubled times and new beginnings can be very scary. But for all that you can't control, as you get up off the mat and move back into life, there is something you can do that will make all the difference in moving on and starting over: giving thanks for those who carried you through the storm and for those who are there to help you begin again.

When you give thanks to those who have been so kind, an attitude of gratitude emerges that helps you reenter life and catapults you from the margins of despair to the center of life and rebirth. As the saying goes, "A door closes, and a window opens." Those who survive trauma or loss often say it is because they found the fortitude to grieve for their loss and then push forward to begin again.

Here, you can see how after darkness there comes a dawn and

a new beginning. Finding gratitude in the unknown, in what lies ahead, can help you shed the burden of the loss to clear space for something better to arrive.

Gratitude Meditation:

THE BLESSING WAY

This tried-and-true meditation has taken many people through the peaks and valleys of life. Innovated by Roberta Baxter, a cancer survivor who was diagnosed and then almost immediately laid off from her job, this mantra will move you from anxiety and worry to peaceful positivity. Whenever Roberta had a "monkey mind" moment and began "angsting," she would say to herself, "I trust in the universe. I am blessed. I am healing and whole. Abundance and all good things surround me, the universe will provide, my life is getting better each and every day." Roberta would speak this mantra aloud and even scribble it on coffee napkins. Soon her friends began to incorporate her affirmations into their own lives, taking note of the affirmations' calming and restorative effects. Roberta has since compiled other fragile, albeit helpful and hopeful, "homemade affirmations" to get through trying times. Use hers or create your own verbal meditations to help you with any one of life's difficult moments.

ROBERTA'S CLASSIC HOMEMADE AFFIRMATIONS

"Each day brings new opportunities to learn and grow; for that I am grateful."

"I am surrounded by love: we are here on the planet to give and receive as much love as we can."

Roberta still scribbles on napkins but also places self-affirmations into her smartphone, which come to her as reminders with a lovely little ringing chime!

GETTING THROUGH THE *BARDOS*

The Buddhists believe in reincarnation, that death is but a step in the soul's continuing journey. The purpose of a *Sukhavti* ceremony is to help guide the newly dead spirit through the *bardos*, a continuum through which the spirit must pass. Safe passage is not guaranteed, for the deceased must get past Tibetan demons of terrible aspect. At the service, to help the deceased through the *bardos*, people should say sweet things, sad things, funny things, and extremely honest things about the loved one. In fact, it is of the utmost importance to be very frank and tell the truth, as it is this honesty that will best help the spirit through the *bardos*.

Steps for a Successful Sukhavti

1. Gather Tibetan temple incense and flowers, and invite people to a room set up for meditation with floor mats and pillows. If possible, invite the newly dead person's spiritual teacher or someone well acquainted with both Tibetan Buddhism and the subject of the service.

2. Begin with a statement of purpose of the *Sukhavti* for those who have never attended one, followed by a 10-minute silent meditation.

3. Light incense and place it together with flowers in front of a photo or image of the newly dead person.

4. Invite anyone who has anything to say about the person to speak, explaining the helpfulness of truth and honesty in aiding the spirit through the bardos. The serene nature of this Buddhist ceremony allows for silence and reflection: speaking should not be forced.

In this look at life's passages, we have made the journey from birth to death and many phases in between. The more rituals you create and perform to acknowledge these phases of human life, the richer your life will be.

Gratitude Exercise:

COUNT YOUR BLESSINGS

Make your own gratitude list at the beginning of each month. While your list may change slightly throughout the year, there will be constants for which you are always grateful. After a few months have gone by, review your list for changes and patterns. What are you always thankful for? What changes? Are you grateful mostly for your relationships? Your family? Your job? Your town? In what areas of your life does gratitude seem to be lacking?

Gratitude Practice:

CREATING MORE TIME

Embrace the questions. As you look ahead, ask yourself what you hope to be a year from now. What do you need to live the joyous, creative new life you hope for? What do you need to change? Use this quotation from Rainer Maria Rilke as your mantra:

"Be patient toward all that is unsolved in your heart and try to love the questions themselves."

THE GIFT OF BREATH

Find a yoga class near you. Experiment as you go through the yoga practice. Be open to whatever happens when you venture out and experiment with yoga as a way to heal body, mind, and spirit. And be grateful for those moments.

MORNING PRAYER

Start each day with the *Modeh Ani*—a Jewish morning prayer:

I am thankful before You,
Living and Sustaining Ruler,
Who returned my soul to me with mercy.
Your faithfulness is great.

Give thanks for a little and you will find a lot.

—THE HAUSA OF NIGERIA

WRITE YOUR LIFE

Take full account of the excellencies which you possess, and in gratitude remember how you would hanker after them, if you had them not.

—MARCUS AURELIUS

When a person doesn't have gratitude, something is missing in his or her humanity. A person can almost be defined by his or her attitude toward gratitude.

—ELIE WIESEL

....

....

....

....

....

....

....

....

Gratitude is a vaccine, an antitoxin,
and an antiseptic.

– JOHN HENRY TOWETT

....

....

....

....

....

....

....

....

....

....

The Good News:

HONORING DAILY GLIMPSES OF GRATITUDE

It was during one of life's toughest times that Vikki Smith decided she would focus on the good in her life.

So during her divorce from her husband of twenty-seven years, the Austin, Texas, mom of two kids, ages 21 and 23, knew her life was going to change in many ways when her husband moved out.

That is when she began writing every night in a "grateful" journal. "I keep it on my bedside table, and before turning out my light each night, I make a point to list something for which I'm grateful," Vicki says. "Some days I have ten things—normally, this is when I manage to get in bed earlier and have more time—and some days I'm exhausted and can only manage to get one or two things written down. I do not limit myself and find that sometimes I'm repetitive or very general. I might write that I am grateful for healthy children, a roof over my head, or health insurance."

But she also likes to be more specific to the day. "I might write that I am grateful to find the kitchen clean when I returned home from work this evening. (My sons have moved back home while finishing up college.)"

Recently, her entry was this: "I am grateful to find some little blossoms have pushed through the tangled mess that is my front garden. Despite all my efforts to impede it by my negligence, the garden, too, was determined to be grateful for spring and the opportunity to bloom anew."

It is easy to be disgruntled daily—there will always be challenges that block our way to achieving our goals or desires. Writing in her journal helps Vicki remember that "the true joys in life come from recognizing the gift in each moment—not in the final hour."

Gratitude Power Tools:

GRACE IN GETTING THROUGH
THE TOUGH STUFF

Our editor for *Living Life as a Thank You* also worked on Tony Burrough's book, *The Code: Ten Intentions for a Better World*. She credits getting a great new home, job, and increased happiness by using the methods in his book. She observed that gratitude is a key tenet in the code as well. Have a look at Tony's "intention process." The wisdom herein has helped hundreds of thousands of people; you might be the next.

THE INTENTION PROCESS
INFORMATION SHEET

Our thoughts create our experiences.

Saying our intentions out loud focuses our thoughts.

There is power in the spoken word.

Positive thoughts bring positive experiences.

Negative thoughts bring undesired experiences.

It's important to trust and know that the things that we intend are coming to us because doubt will interfere with the manifestation of our positive intentions.

We always ask that in order for our intentions to come to us, they must serve the highest and best good for the Universe and the highest and best good for ourselves and others.

As we go around the Circle, we express gratitude for intentions that have come to us and we state our new intentions.

The power of the Intention Circle arises from everyone supporting everyone else's intentions.

CLARITY IS IMPORTANT.

We eliminate such words as trying, hoping, wanting, to be, and not

We say things in a positive way: for example, instead of "I intend that I am not afraid anymore," we say "I intend that I am courageous."

We don't name sicknesses in our Circles; we see everyone in their Highest Light.

We say our intentions daily, and we gather together once a week.

We don't know when or how our intentions will manifest for us; we just know that they will!

We always end our intentions with our seven favorite words: So be it and so it is !

Finding the Light in Dark Days

Sometimes we feel deflated or overwhelmed, someone or something hurts us or disappoints us, or we hear bad news about a loved one's medical condition. On those days, when you feel your light has gone out, remember there is always a glimmer of hope and something to be thankful for. Albert Schweitzer said it well:

"Sometimes our light goes out, but is blown again into instant flame by an encounter with another human being. Each of us owes the deepest thanks to those who have rekindled this inner light."

DON'T JUST GO THROUGH IT, GROW THROUGH IT

An attitude of gratitude can make a profound difference in our day-to-day lives, yet, as we all come to know, not every day is filled with all good things. We each endure difficult passages: illnesses, money trouble, work woes, relationship issues, the loss of a loved one, and countless others. These are the vicissitudes of life. However, it is the attitude you bring to each situation that makes all the difference.

1. *What is the most difficult thing you have dealt with in your life so far? How do you feel you handled it?*

....

....

....

....

....

....

....

....

2. *Who in your life is presently going through a tough time? What can you offer?*

....

....

....

....

....

....

3. *Name a person you know who handles life's challenges with an enviable grace? What can you learn from him or her?*

....

....

....

....

....

....

Six

THE POWER OF GRATITUDE
TO MAKE A DIFFERENCE IN THE WORLD

Anyone who sets out to make a real change in the world has to start somewhere. Typically, change is an incremental, snowballing process. Often, the best place to start is in your own community—think global, act local, as the saying goes. Many cities all over the country have a dire need for volunteers at shelters and kitchens for the needy, so why not start there?

Our highest purpose is to give to others. When you do, gratitude becomes contagious—reaching out not only fuels the collective power of gratitude, but this simple act of giving thanks and giving back can change the world. Those people who use their bounty and their spirit of thankfulness to reach out and help others inspire us. It doesn't matter what your circumstances are; there is no better way to rise above them than to volunteer to help a charitable organization, mentor someone, or give counsel and support to someone who needs it. Your own thankfulness can manifest itself in your actions and deeds, in the choice to share your gifts and abundance with those in need. And evidence suggests that helping others may be as important to your physical well-being as is regular exercise and proper nutrition.

In fact, numerous studies have shown that people who volunteer have lower rates of mortality and depression and higher functional ability. Two studies in particular indicate that there is a threshold of about 100 hours per year of volunteer activity, or about 2 hours per week, required to achieve a health benefit. According to Stephen Post—director of the Institute for Research on Unlimited Love, a Case Western Reserve University research group that focuses on the scientific study of altruism, compassion, and service—you don't have to do anything dramatic. "It starts with a shift from thinking *I am the center of the world* to a willingness to act toward others in helpful ways," Post says.

Gratitude Meditation:

SERVICE

"To Be of Use," Marge Piercy's marvelous poem, suggests something of the human condition—that we all long to be useful, to help, to work together toward a common goal. This is surely the best part of the human spirit. Meditate on this:

What is my true purpose? What am I here to do in this life?

We recommend that you contemplate this question deeply and for a very long time—days, weeks, months, and years even. Let the answer speak through your service to others.

NO STRINGS ATTACHED

Write down the things that someone has given you, no strings attached, for which you are grateful. It can be an old sofa, some sound advice, or a lift to the airport. Now list ten things that you would like to give someone yourself, and see how many of those things you can cross off in a week.

Examples

      Baby-sit for a relative

      Buy a friend a cup of coffee

      Volunteer at a soup kitchen

1. ....

....

....

2. ....

....

....

3.

4.

5.

6.

7.

8. ....
....
....

9. ....
....
....

10. ....
....
....

Gratitude Practice:

PLANET POSITIVE

Because the world we live in today is very much about getting in your head and staying there, many of us have to make a concentrated effort to become grounded and in touch with our bodies and the natural world around us. Grounding is the technique for centering you within your being, getting into your body and out of your head. Grounding is the way we reconnect and balance ourselves though the power of the element of earth. When you see someone driving past talking on their cell phone, you know that they are not grounded. For deep grounding, we recommend a creative visualization or, better yet, a group guided meditation.

This is the simplest of rituals, one you can do every day of your life. As you walk, take the time to look and really see what is in your path. For example, my friend Eileen takes a bag with her and picks up every piece of garbage in her path. She does this as an act of love for the Earth. During the ten years she has practiced this ritual, she has probably turned a mountain of garbage into recycled glass, paper, and plastic.

TAKING THE OPPORTUNITY TO GIVE

When we were children, many of us were schooled to associate saying "Thank you" with obligation and even guilt.

Your parents might have said to you, "Say, 'Thank you,' to Grandma for the pajamas" or "When I was a child I was reminded that many children in the world went hungry while we always had three square meals a day. Look at everything you have that you take for granted."

Invariably, many of us carried this idea of saying "Thank you" as an obligation into adulthood, and these memories can cause you to feel an underlying sense of resentment when you owe someone a thank-you or feel that someone has not sufficiently thanked you. There is a not-so-subtle feeling of obligation either way.

But, ironically, giving and gratitude often take us by surprise. Often, you will find that it is through your own giving that you receive. And when you realize this, you feel so thankful for the shift—for the light that comes on in your mind and the surprising sense of well-being you acquire through your giving.

Sometimes, it was your earliest mentors who taught you the lessons on new beginnings that you need to relearn time and again.

Take some time to thank a teacher today. If your child is in school, you can write a letter to her teacher. Tell him what you appreciate about him and how your child appreciates him. Send a "report card" to the principal expressing what a great job this teacher is doing, or honor a school by adopting a classroom and purchasing supplies, or buy books for the library. You can go to www.teacherscount.org for more ideas.

Ultimately, man should not ask what the meaning of his life is, but rather must recognize that it is he who is asked. In a word, each man is questioned by life; and he can only answer to life by answering for his own life; to life he can only respond by being responsible.

—MAN'S SEARCH FOR MEANING,
BY VIKTOR FRANKL

WRITE YOUR LIFE

Life is full of beauty. Notice it. Notice the bumblebee, the small child, and the smiling faces. Smell the rain, and feel the wind. Live your life to the fullest potential, and fight for your dreams.

—Ashley Smith

....

....

....

....

....

....

....

....

Gratefulness drives out alienation, there is no room in the heart for both. When you are grateful, you say yes to belonging and you reach out to share your gratitude with others through volunteering and putting gratefulness into action. Gratitude strengthens—caring for others is draining, but grateful caregivers are healthier than less grateful ones.

—BROTHER DAVID STEINDL-RAST

It takes a person of great heart to see...
the wisdom the elders have to offer,
and so serve them out of gratitude for
the life they have passed on to us.

—KEN NERBURN

....

....

....

....

....

....

....

....

The dream begins with a teacher who believes in you, who tugs and pushes and leads you to the next plateau, sometimes poking you with a sharp stick called "truth."

—DAN RATHER

Healing Planet Earth: Green and Grateful

On Earth Day 2008, Karen Talavera, a Palm Beach County, Florida, writer, mom, and marketing professional, remembers asking herself, "Wouldn't it be great if we could use gratitude to help create a better Earth? To help heal the catastrophic environmental destruction we've inflicted in merely a century?"

So she came up with a powerful proposal.

While there are thousands, if not tens of thousands, of Earth Day events planned worldwide, Karen recommends one that is the easiest to participate in and perhaps the most universal. It's called "10 Minutes of Gratitude for Planet Earth." This is what you do:

On Earth Day, at 12:00 noon in your time zone, sit quietly for 10 minutes and think of all the places, experiences, and moments of earthly nature you have ever enjoyed, and be grateful for them. This event is not intended to be a simultaneous, central gathering in one place; it will happen everywhere at noon in each time zone. People may certainly gather together in groups if they wish.

Yep, that's it. You don't have to go anywhere, give any money, or receive any solicitations. It's a seemingly simple idea, but think of the chain of gratitude that could be created if everyone took the time to test Karen's idea.

Helping Hands

What is a Friend? When a friend says, "I need you!" what
do you say?

Do you say, "What happened?" or do you say, "How can I
help?"

Does it really matter what happened—or does it matter only
that your friend needs you, and has asked for your help?

God never asks us—"What happened?"

He says: "I love you—I am your friend!"

THE COURAGE TO SERVE

One of the women we admire the most in this world is Texan Jackie Waldman. Though Jackie suffers from multiple sclerosis, she handles it with grace and aplomb. She always stays positive and, more important, she thinks of others and not just her own situation. She went on the hunt for others' good news stories, amassing an astonishing collection of tales of people simply giving. My favorite of her stories is about "The Peanut Butter Lady," Bea Salazar. A single mother struggling to care for her own young children, Bea endured her biggest setback when she was severely injured at her work. She was left with intense pain, which she still battles daily, and was unable to continue working. Her accident left her feeling depressed, hopeless, and desperate, but thanks to a caring social worker she was able to forge ahead and continue to recover, and eventually, she was able to do more around the house and with her children. One day, while taking out the trash she saw a small boy rummaging through a dumpster for food. Shocked, Bea took the child to her home and made him a peanut butter sandwich and sent him back home. Later when she heard a soft knock at her door, she opened it to find another scruffy little boy, skinny and disheveled. The boy sheepishly asked, "Is it true you're giving peanut butter sand-wiches away?" Always one to open her heart, Bea fed the young boy as well and sent him home. The next day when Bea heard a knock at her door, there were thirteen more hungry kids. It was then that Bea realized her calling, and from a loaf of bread and a jar of peanut butter grew a small but important program to feed the local children. Both Jackie and "The Peanut Butter Lady" have been on *Oprah* four times, and they continue to serve their community through their Angel network. Could you do something similar?

....

....

....

....

....

....

....

....

"AND IN THE END THE LOVE YOU TAKE IS EQUAL TO THE LOVE YOU MAKE"

1. *Have you volunteered recently for a food bank or a soup kitchen? If so, how did this make you feel?*

....

....

....

....

....

....

2. *Short of travelling to Haiti, where can you serve? What needs can you address in your own back yard?*

....

....

....

....

....

3. *Have you received significant help in your life? (Haven't we all!) When was it? What did it mean to you? Have you properly thanked the person or people who helped you? Even if it was last week or 20 years ago, pick up the phone (no e-mails, texts, or Facebooking!) and express your true gratitude.*

Seven

FINDING GRACE AND WISDOM IN GOODBYES

Life intends Life. There is no death that is not another life beginning. There is no end that does not start anew. In every loss, in every grief, there is the hand of comfort, the hand of faith, waiting to move forward into new ways.

—JULIA CAMERON

To be certain, as part of humanity you will face heavy hits—bumps in the road that are the harsh realities of life. The truth of the matter is, life is not always fair. But in the midst of this suffering and pain, you have a choice: you can give in to your sadness and anger, and give up, or you can affirm life and the extraordinary power of grace of which humans are capable.

The challenge then is this: how do you find the unexpected blessings in difficult or challenging times? How do you reframe goodbyes and loss as a doorway, an entrance to the new?

While these may seem like difficult tasks—especially living in a culture where complaining is an art form and lack of appreciation a bad habit—there are some to whom gratitude comes quite naturally.

These people are able to see the glass as half-full, and following their lead might help the rest of us to cultivate their same approach to life.

Cari Stein, a glass-half-full resident of Baltimore, believes that her desire to nurture an "attitude of gratitude" is sincere and honest. Cari has experienced firsthand how gratitude not only changes her outlook and mood—it truly changes circumstances. What seems at the time a horrible stroke of bad luck can became an event for which we are eternally grateful.

This "horrible stroke of bad luck" came in the form of an infection for Cari, only a few weeks after she had taken a new position, her dream job in TV production in Baltimore. Ignoring her symptoms because she was so busy with her new job only worsened her condition and ultimately landed her in the hospital. But instead of checking into a local hospital, Cari decided to go back home to Brooklyn and receive care in a hospital closer to her parents. The few weeks she spent there recovering, she was also able to spend quality time with her parents. "We played board games, cards, and talked about life," she fondly remembers. "It turned out to be a very special time in my life."

But what made it even more significant and poignant than she ever could have imagined was that a few months later, her mother died of a heart attack. Had Cari not fallen ill, she would have missed out on all those special moments she shared with her parents. She understood that she had been given the gift of time with her mom, her best friend. What had appeared to be adversity became a blessing.

Dealing with the loss of a loved one can be the most trying and difficult time for even the strongest of people, but you can seek solace, reconciling your sadness and loss, in gratitude.

Everyone struggles with the act of letting go—whether it's physically letting go of material goods, emotionally detaching from people who have hurt you, losing a job, or saying goodbye and moving on when someone you love has died. Sometimes gratitude is less about striving than it is about surrendering.

Difficult though it may be to understand, it is gratitude that gets you through these stressful times and painful endings. Learning to say, "Thank you," even when it feels forced, can go a long way. Being grateful helps you stop trying to control what will inevitably happen and unlocks positive energy in your life. Sadness and loss can become blessings and bring unexpected gifts. In giving thanks for the past, you then are able to move forward into the present.

Gratitude Meditation:

LET GO TO HOLD ON

Start your day with this intention from *The Language of Letting Go* by Melody Beattie:

> Today, I will be grateful. I will start the process of turning today's pain into tomorrow's joy.

Gratitude Exercise:

MEMORY MARKER

Acknowledging the end of a life is an important part of the healing process. It is necessary to honor this life passing both psychologically and emotionally. This exercise contains carefully considered questions for you to ask yourself—we recommend you give this a great deal of thought; the deepest level of introspection, as you will be bidding farewell to an important part of your life, doubtless, that brought you much joy before the sorrow. Many emotions are going to rise. You can gently and with love put the feelings to rest.

1. *What did this person mean to you?*

....

....

....

....

2. *What are the memories you wish to treasure and keep?*

....

....

....

3. How did this person bring you joy and meaning?

....

....

....

....

4. What is your gratitude towards this person?

....

....

....

....

Write down the precious memories and put them in a safe place.
Now, concentrate on making *new* happy memories.

1. ....

....

....

2. ....

....

....

3. ....

....

....

4. ....

....

....

5. ....

....

6.

7.

8.

9.

10.

AFTER THOUGHTS

Create a prayer of farewell for a person in your life who is leaving, and a thank-you for what they have meant in your life. With each thank-you, acknowledge a gift that this person has given you. *Example:* "Thank you, Dad, for being such a good listener. Thank you, Dad, for giving me the gift of loving to read." Then say, "We know that God goes with you."

THE CIRCLE OF LIFE

Christian writer G. K. Chesterton had the right idea when he said we need to get in the habit of "taking things with gratitude and not taking things for granted." Write a letter to your relatives acknowledging the special role a relative who is now gone has played in your family circle. Ask them to say a prayer of thanksgiving for this person and the legacy he or she has left for all of you.

DOMO ARIGATO

Try the Japanese gratitude practice called *Naikan*, which means "looking inside." Practitioners claim that it helps people understand themselves and their relationships and put things into better perspective. Cari Stein was able to find the gift in her situation. Can you do the same?

The practice involves asking yourself these three questions:

1. What have I received from this person?

2. What have I given to this person?

3. What troubles and difficulties have I caused to this person?

....

....

....

....

....

....

....

....

....

....

Find the good—and praise it.

—ALEX HALEY

WRITE YOUR LIFE

Gratitude is the memory of the heart.

—Jean-Baptiste Massieu

....

....

....

....

....

....

....

....

....

I awoke this morning with devout thanksgiving for my friends, the old and the new.

—RALPH WALDO EMERSON

....

....

....

....

....

....

....

....

....

Gratitude is our most direct line to God and the angels. If we take the time, no matter how crazy and troubled we feel, we can find something to be thankful for. The more we seek gratitude, the more reason the angels will give us for gratitude and joy to exist in our lives.

—TERRY LYNN TAYLOR

Gratitude as a Second Chance

Dorothea Hover-Kramer, a psychotherapist and author of six books, including *Second Chance at Your Dream: Engaging Your Body's Energy Resources for Optimal Aging, Creativity and Health,* believes in the transformative power of gratitude.

She says, "Being thankful changes our energy from demanding to appreciation. Instead of increasing our expectations of how things should be, we can move toward recognizing what is. I like learning from my pets—every caring gesture or morsel of food is appreciated. It's important to stay in touch with the reality of how much we've been given!"

Gratitude Power Tools:

GRACE NOTES

Write a goodbye note to someone who is no longer in your life. In this note, write down the five greatest memories you have of your time together and give thanks for them. As you recount the profound effect this person had on you, try to think of ways in which you are a better person for having known this special friend, lover, or relative. Imagine how you would be without having known this person, and be grateful for the impact he or she had on you.

....

....

....

....

....

....

....

....

HAPPY ENDINGS

Our favorite wisdom regarding death stems from a Native American belief, that your death will be as you lived, and in the end, it matters not how much money or possessions you had, but how kind you were to people.

1. *How do you want to be regarded after you have "passed on"?*

....

....

....

....

....

2. *Are you "kind enough" to have a "good death"?*

....

....

....

....

....

3. *If not, what might you do to change your legacy?*

....
....
....
....
....
....
....
....
....
....
....

Eight

INSPIRATION AND PERSPIRATION:
ALL PARTS GRATITUDE

Daring deeds and great accomplishments often start with a light bulb moment—a bright idea that takes hold and illuminates our path. Whether we start on our journey full of appreciation or embark on one to seek inspiration and fulfillment, gratitude is the driving force that brings us closer to our goals. It is the one thing upon which we can all rely, not only to push us along but also to encourage us and give us direction when our paths become uncertain or unclear. Writer Alan Kaufman, despite encountering many of life's difficult obstacles, is sure to keep this in mind as he continues along his journey—stalwart, pensive, unimpeded, and always with a grateful heart.

THE JOURNEYMAN
by Alan Kaufman

Each morning, at the thought of the effort that I must expend to fully be myself and feel completely alive, my body tires and heart balks, the mind protests and ingrained self-defeating patterns flare up, promising me the old, familiar rewards of illusory safety and the numbness of thwarted growth.

Only my spirit stands apart from these deceptions and gently whispering, beckons me to the place of magical possibility.

Each morning, I follow. I know that I awake the same person whom I was before I ever undertook becoming the person I truly am. And so I rise and choose not to revisit my well-furnished rut but dare to advance, through conscious, principled, and disciplined actions, into mystery and the unknown, where the person I am already exists, waiting to be claimed.

I think of myself as a journeyman with a portable spiritual tool kit. In the old days, the journeyman carpenter or housebuilder was willing to travel in any direction to provide his services, so long as the trip did not require more than 24 hours of travel.

For me, each 24 hour day is a journey I set forth, bearing my spiritual tools. For those hours, I will seek to be of service and to practice gratitude in the world that I encounter.

But my performances are always, always less than perfect, and sometimes they are quite close to disasters! It is easy then to feel so discouraged that you stand ready to abandon the way.

There are no failures but one: to believe your mind when it tells you that you're hopeless, that you'll never succeed, and to give up.

True inner transformation is beyond success or failure: there is no single success to be attained or failure so great that you are thrown from your path forever. There is only effort that has been creditworthy or instances that require improvement. Monitoring these daily advances and retreats are essential to inner change.

But you must make the effort. You must consciously choose to pick up the tools and use them. You must consciously choose the life of inner freedom and spiritual majesty. You must work for this.

You must struggle and strain. You must walk alone at times. You must show more courage than you thought you had. You must sacrifice time and sometimes pleasures. For as the world is, you are the only hero of your story and only you and no other can make the narrative of your true destiny.

You are right now a beautiful success, simply for having chosen this path, which will never abandon you. Sometimes sprinting and sometimes stumbling, at times straying but then returning, just so long as you know where inner transformation lies and are advancing with renewed determination, you will find realms of mystery and miracle, truth and authenticity. And each day that you choose this path will manifest your glory.

Gratitude Meditation:

MIND OVER *MATTERS*

As the saying goes, only you can change yourself. And to achieve real change takes sustained effort and hard work. True transformation will not happen unless you roll up your sleeves and commit to the tough stuff that is inner work. If you are a little disturbed by some of the answers and questions you are working though in this workbook process, that is *good*. There should be some real sweat, a little sleeplessness and intensity in your soul searching. Inspiration only comes after a lot of perspiration.

Focusing your mind is surely one of the very best ways to prepare for hard inner work.

> Put aside all worries and decide which quality or self-improvement goal you want. Write it down on a piece of paper. Sit on the floor or at a table with the paper in front of you. For example, it might say, "Be more forgiving" or "Stop procrastinating." Close your eyes and see the words in your mind. Say it a few times: "I forgive." Picture who or what you want to forgive. Now take the paper and write the list of forgiveness. Focus on it, and then, let the forgiving begin.

Gratitude Exercise:

LIVING YOUR STORY

Create a "Life List Journal." This is different from a bucket list. It is a record of your daily life, written in a biographical style, or in the manner of a memoir. For this, you should speak to your aspirations—hopes, dreams, and fears. Is anything holding you back? Ferret out the psychic obstacles and work them out in your journal. Carry it with you, as once the process has begun, it will accelerate and your personal growth will be astounding.

Gratitude Practice:

REWRITE TO BE RIGHT

Try "rewriting your life." Consider that you know who you are, how you react, what triggers you. You might even warn other people about the ways you are, or quietly wait for them to figure it out. But what if you could create yourself new every day? What if you could start saying things about yourself that create you as more of who you want to be? Maybe you can. We invite you to take it on. For just one week, pick a way of being that perhaps you don't think you are and start affirming that way. Let's say, for example, I am beautiful or I am generous. Pick one that you aspire to be but don't think you are quite there yet.

Now, for a whole week, really take on practicing being this way. Look yourself in the mirror first thing each morning; every time you get into the car, look into that mirror, before you go to sleep at night again, look into the mirror and repeat your affirmation. Keep it up all week long. Notice your experience as the week progresses. Let what you are saying sink in; stop resisting it; just breathe into your words. At the end of the week, ask yourself, "How was that for me? What am I present to now? How do I see and experience myself?"

You can rewrite your life. Whatever story you are telling yourself and others, if it empowers you, great, keep sharing it. If it doesn't empower you, start practicing sharing another story. Make one up that is empowering—you made up one that wasn't, so why not make up one that is? Go ahead, let yourself fall in love with *you*—and with everyone else in your life, too.

....

....

....

....

....

....

....

....

....

....

If you can imagine it, you can achieve it; if you can dream it, you can become it.

—William Arthur Ward

WRITE YOUR LIFE

Silent gratitude isn't much use to anyone.

—G.B. STERN

....

....

....

....

....

....

....

....

....

Not knowing when the dawn will come, I open every door.

—EMILY DICKINSON

....

....

....

....

....

....

....

....

....

....

By saying grace, we release the Divine sparks in our food.

—Rabbi Herschel

....

....

....

....

....

....

....

....

....

The greatest part of our happiness depends on our dispositions, not our circumstances.

—MARTHA WASHINGTON

....

....

....

....

....

....

....

....

....

....

Weather Report

by BJ Gallagher

"Any day I'm vertical
is a good day"
that's what I always say.
And I give thanks
that I'm healthy.
If you ask me,
"How are you?"
I'll answer, "GREAT!"
because in saying so,
I make it so.
And I give thanks
that I can choose my attitude.
When Life gives me dark clouds and rain,
I appreciate the moisture
which brings a soft curl to my hair.
When Life gives me sunshine,
I gratefully turn my face up
to feel its warmth on my cheeks.
When Life brings fog,
I hug my sweater around me
and give thanks for the cool shroud of mystery
that makes the familiar seem different and intriguing.
When Life brings snow,
I dash outside to catch the first flakes on my tongue,
relishing the icy miracle that is a snowflake.
Life's events and experiences
are like the weather—

they come and go,
no matter what my preference.
So, what the heck?!
I might as well decide to enjoy them.
For indeed,
there IS a time for every purpose
under Heaven.
Each season brings its own unique blessings.
And I give thanks.

OFF THE BEATEN PATH

If you travel outside the United States to a developing country, take the time to get out of the resort, off the tourist track, and experience the local culture. Put away your credit card, buy from the locals, talk to the indigenous people, and take note of what makes them happy.

Gratitude Power Tools:

YOUR GOALS WILL GROW *YOU*

Make a list of short-term goals you would like to achieve by the end of the year, month, or even week. As you accomplish your goals, give gratitude for the effort, inspiration, people, and other factors that helped you along the way.

Gratitude Questions:

YOUR SPIRITUAL "BUCKET LIST"

Approaching middle age, many people begin to question the very nature of their being. While many a fancy sports car or other accoutrement have evidenced the classic "midlife crisis," we each have our own way of dealing with the changes. It is an essential part of the maturation process; in fact, if you *don't* feel the restlessness, you definitely have a problem! Our recommendation for this midlife mayhem is to start a list of "evolutionary goals" to abet the inner will that can open you into a wholly integrated person.

1. *What spirituality or wisdom tradition draws you in?*

....

....

....

....

2. *Do you go on retreats?*

....

....

....

3. *If you could go anywhere in the world for a spiritual pilgrimage, where would you go?*

....

....

....

....

4. *If you could ask a question to any spiritual teacher, who would it be? What is the question?*

....

....

....

....

Nine

GRATITUDE IN TIMES OF TRANSITION

What if you gave someone a gift, and they neglected to thank you for it—would you be likely to give them another? Life is the same way. In order to attract more of the blessings that life has to offer, you must truly appreciate what you already have.

—RALPH MARSTON

At some point in our lives, we've all been told to look for the blessings in times of upheaval and confusion, as often is the case when we're ending a relationship, moving to a new job, or facing a life passage. But it is hard in transition not to be pessimistic when the future is so uncertain, or when we've lost something or someone we love.

Transitions can electrify the air with fear. That's because in transitions, you're taking apart the structure of the life you know and preparing to rebuild it into something new.

Unfortunately, the more we focus on our fears and what we don't have in our lives, the scarier and more depressing things get. How can we expect more in the future if we don't appreciate what we already have? Even if something cherished is now missing, we must humble ourselves and look at what we do have to be grateful for. What we are experiencing in transition is temporary, and this too will pass.

When we focus on our blessings and look forward to what lies ahead with a spirit of hope, it can help us mobilize the courage and the heart to open the gates of tenderness, right in the midst of fear and uncertainty. Then we can see transitional times as opportunities for tremendous growth in our lives.

Consider the words of Lee Woodruff, reflecting on the months after her husband, the reporter Bob Woodruff, was injured in Iraq: "Thankfully, there inevitably comes a period in time when you begin to move away from the eye of the hurricane. No matter what the outcome, you let out your breath and learn to operate once again outside of the crisis mode. It's the point in time when you have to put one tentative foot in front of the other and widen the distance between you and the first horrible piece of news."

In times of trouble or transition, when we are feeling down or afraid, the best medicine can be hope and gratitude. To be grateful gives us hope, and hope lets us know that things can get better, that we can move through our journey.

Michele Woodward, a mother of two from Arlington, Virginia, faced her most difficult time of transition when her husband left her for a younger woman he'd met on the Internet. "If you had said, 'This, too, shall pass,' I might have scratched your eyes out," recalls Michele. "If you had urged balance and sangfroid, I would have impaled you on the plumber's helper." Michele was unable to let go of her wallowing and self-pity: "I was more about hurt and revenge than gratitude. Gratitude was way too positive an emotion for me to feel." And then one day, something changed and gratitude found a toehold in her life. "I wasn't paying a ton of attention. Just, one day, there it was: gentle glimmers of gratitude. I bid a cautious welcome and began counting the ways I was grateful. Just one a day to start, then two, then three—then a whole lot. A slew of gratitude graced my consciousness," she recounts. Michele became grateful that she was no longer with a man who could not be faithful, that she was no longer centering her life on someone who did not return the favor. Michele has since learned that "even if the worst thing you could possibly imagine has happened to you, because you are not alone, because you are loved, you will pass the test. And that's something to be grateful for."

Gratitude Meditation:

CHANGE YOUR LIFE

Let's face it—change is very, very hard. Or is it? Well, that all depends on your perspective. There are certain changes and new phases of life that are challenging: aging parents who require more time and care, economic woes, health issues; the lengthy list goes on. However, how you decide to greet the coming changes is what makes all the difference. A certain "flexibility of attitude" is required to handle change well. So next time a life transition appears on your plate, try this mediation.

First, visualize being enveloped by a golden glow. Feel the warmth and protection this aura provides. If a friend or loved one is experiencing a difficult challenge, include them in this protective golden shield of love and light, as well. When you regard others in such a tender, caring way, they can feel this love and its benefits.

Gratitude Exercise:

THE BEST CASE SCENARIO HANDBOOK

We've talked about managing difficult transitional times, but it can be quite illuminating to consider the opposite—what could be the best thing that could possibly happen to you? Write down a list of "best case scenarios" that could happen to you and your loved ones, and then visualize how these things might come to fruition.

1. ....

   ....

   ....

2. ....

   ....

   ....

3. ....

   ....

   ....

   ....

4.

5.

6.

7.

8.

"I WANNA THANK YOU"

Lee Brower, founder and CEO of Empowered Wealth LC, collects and gives away "gratitude rocks." He advises people to put one in their pocket, and every time they touch it take a moment to think about something they're grateful for.

SELF-BLESSINGS

Try this *mudra* (a yogic hand gesture) that is a way to bless yourself and remind yourself that you are protected and loved. Hold your thumb and your first two fingers together and circle your heart while you chant, "One Earth, one people, and one love." Repeat as many times as you want. It reminds you that you are one with the Earth and the people who love you.

CONSCIOUS WELL-BEING

Practice this suggestion from Alan Cohen whenever life throws you a curveball.

When confronted with a situation that appears fragmented or impossible, step back, close your eyes, and envision perfection where you saw brokenness. Go to the inner place where there is no problem, and abide in the consciousness of well-being.

Gratitude unlocks the fullness of life. It turns what we have into enough, and more. It turns denial into acceptance, chaos into order, and confusion into clarity. It turns problems into gifts, failures into success, the unexpected into perfect timing, and mistakes into important events. Gratitude makes sense of our past, brings peace for today, and creates a vision for tomorrow.

—MELODY BEATTIE

WRITE YOUR LIFE

Praise the bridge that carried you over.

—GEORGE COLMAN

....

....

....

....

....

....

....

....

....

....

....

He is a wise man who does not grieve for the things which he has not, but rejoices for those which he has.

—Epictetus

....

....

....

....

....

....

....

....

....

Whenever you find tears in your eyes, especially unexpected tears, it is well to pay the closest attention. They are not only telling the secret of who you are, but more often than not of the mystery of where you have come from and are summoning you to where you should go next.

—FREDERICK BUECHNER

Ten Ways to Cultivate a Grateful Heart

1. Be grateful and recognize the things others have done to help you.

2. When you say, "Thank you," to someone, it signals what you appreciate and why you appreciate it.

3. Post a "Thank you to all" on your Facebook page or your blog, or send individual e-mails to friends, family, and colleagues.

4. Send a handwritten thank-you note. These are note-worthy because so few of us take time to write and mail them.

5. Think thoughts of gratitude—two or three good things that happened today—and notice calm settle through your head, at least for a moment. It activates a part of the brain that floods the body with endorphins, or feel-good hormones.

6. Remember the ways your life has been made easier or better because of others' efforts. Be aware of and acknowledge the good things, large and small, going on around you.

7. Keep a gratitude journal or set aside time each day or evening to list the people or things you're grateful for today. The list may start out short, but it will grow as you notice more of the good things around you.

8. Being grateful shakes you out of self-absorption and helps you recognize those who've done wonderful things for you. Expressing that gratitude continues to draw those people into your sphere.

9. Remember this thought from Maya Angelou: "When you learn, teach; when you get, give."

10. Join forces to do good. If you have survived illness or loss, you may want to reach out to others to help as a way of showing gratitude for those who reached out to you.

Gratitude Power Tools:

CATCH THEM IF YOU CAN

During difficult transitions, our natural tendency is often to contract and grow rigid. In this state we seem to only be able to focus on the negatives. We think about the despair and torment of the death of a loved one, but not the wonderful moments spent together. We think of the heartbreak of a relationship ending, but not of the exhilaration and freedom of being unattached. We might even scold our loved ones, or our friends, or coworkers for something minor or insignificant when we wallow in such negativity. But it is in these moments specifically that gratitude can be used to alter this way of thinking. Finding positives and accentuating them is the easiest way to turn those proverbial frowns upside down and gray skies back to blue. Try catching someone doing something right for a change, not something wrong. Giving praise for a job well done lifts all parties involved and is the easiest way to say, "Thank You," without actually having to say it.

Gratitude Questions:

CHANGE IS HARD

1. *What has been your life's most difficult transition?*

....

....

2. *Was it forced upon you or initiated by you?*

....

....

3. *How did you cope with the transition?*

....

....

4. *If you could do it differently, how would you?*

....

....

Ten

PUTTING GRATITUDE INTO ACTION

As we express our gratitude, we must never forget that the highest appreciation is not to utter words, but to live by them.

—JOHN FITZGERALD KENNEDY

Throughout this book, you have learned that in both good times and times of uncertainty, you can be inspired by or take solace in the hope that gratitude brings to your life. For those of you who feel fortunate today as you consider the imprint that thankfulness has made, look ahead with a tremendous sense of gratitude.

You've learned from the wealth of inspirational and heartwarming examples how gratitude can make a difference—and can actually change the direction of your life. Let these stories inspire you to live with gratitude each and every day.

Just think what our world would be like if we all adopted an attitude of gratitude in every arena of our lives—at home, at the office, at the grocery store, in chance encounters with strangers.

Studies have shown that even businesses thrive and grow with a touch of thankfulness added to the product mix. In one experiment, a jewelry store owner who called and thanked each of his customers showed a 70 percent increase in purchases. By comparison, those whose customers were told about a sale showed only a 30 percent increase in purchases, and customers who were not thanked did not show an increase in buying behavior.

What you can learn from this is that just as you create an exercise plan for your health, or map out recipes for healthy eating, you need to put gratitude first—literally, and create a daily ritual for giving thanks.

"Build it and they will come," "Seeing is believing," and other similar sayings give life to the idea that in practicing gratitude and saying "Thank you" for what *is*, you create what can *be*.

Katie Mattson is a firm believer that you can be or do anything you want. You just need to intentionally put your beliefs out there for them to manifest. She does this as part of an annual tradition: creating a gratitude dream board. Here, she shares her tools for tapping into the hidden power of gratitude and counting blessings even before they happen.

First, Katie has a self-actualization tool she uses to visualize what she wants to achieve and what she anticipates being grateful for. At the beginning of each year, she creates a dream board and uses it to keep track of her progress, attitude, and goals for the coming 12 months. Using magazines, words, and markers, she maps out what she wants for herself that year.

Katie starts by grabbing a stack of magazines and cutting out words that resonate with her. She advises, "Want to increase your salary this year? Write down a number. Want to lose weight this year? How much? Want to fall in love? What is he or she like? Want to buy a house? What does it look like? Be as specific as possible with your dream board." Initially she purchased a standard poster board and just filled it up. More recently, she purchased a sectioned frame that can be refilled each year.

Each section is used for a different area of her life. "I use phrases and photos of things I want for myself this year: attitudes, empowerment phrases, making natural easy-flowing choices, personal mantras," she says. "In one of the sections I detailed the adventures I'd like to have this year, since traveling to see new places is really important to me. In another, I detailed what I wanted for my business. In the last, what I wanted in the way of love from family, friends, and a future partner."

Katie recommends being creative: "Each day you can get into that grateful feeling place for 'having' each one of these. From there, as they begin to manifest themselves in your life, your gratitude skyrockets and your effort begin to double."

By continuing to embrace gratitude and live in a state of conscious contentment, you may find a path to happiness and joy, and this can inspire others around you. A study published in the *British Medical Journal* by scientists from Harvard University and University of California, San Diego showed that happiness can spread through social networks of family members, friends, and neighbors. Knowing someone who is happy makes you 15.3 percent more likely to be happy yourself, the study found. A happy friend of a friend increases your odds of happiness by 9.8 percent, and even your neighbor's sister's friend can give you a 5.6 percent boost.

Nicholas A. Christakis, MD, a physician and medical sociologist at Harvard who cowrote the study, found that your emotional state is affected by the actions and choices of other people, many of whom you don't even know. Gratitude really can change the world!

Gratitude Meditation:

HEART STEPS

In her book *Heart Steps: Prayers and Declarations for a Creative Life*, Julia Cameron suggests that we experiment with prayers and declarations and then record for ourselves the results we observe in our life and in our consciousness. In your contemplative time, think about the kind of prayer that works for you.

Practice repeating this meditational mantra to yourself every day: "I find joy in service. I open my mind and heart to the plan of service that brings the most joy to me and others. I accept my guidance and direction as they unfold within me." Make note of what really helps you and keep with that direction. May these "heart steps" quicken your own.

Gratitude Exercise:

GRATITUDE HIT LIST

Create a Top Ten list of the things you are most grateful for in your life. Carry it with you in your purse or pocket or post it on your mirror, your refrigerator, or at your office to remind you daily what you are grateful for. These thank-you's will leap off the page at the times when you most need the reminder.

1. ....

....

2. ....

....

3. ....

....

4. ....

....

....

5.

6.

7.

8.

9.

10.

Gratitude Practice:

MANTRA MOMENTS

Say, "Thank you," as many times a day as you can. It will become a daily, moment-to-moment mantra of life. Try keeping tab: What's your day's record? Thank you for everything!

DREAM A LITTLE DREAM

Create a gratitude dream board. Be specific with your goals. When your board is complete, write the phrase, "This or something better is making its way into my life right now. I trust the Universe's plan for me." Then put it up where you can see it, or where you can take it out to look at each day. Many people prefer placing it by their bed, on their bathroom wall, or on the refrigerator. Sweet dreams!

From what we get, we can make a living; what we give, however, makes a life.

—ARTHUR ASHE

WRITE YOUR LIFE

God gave you a gift of 86,400 sec-
onds today. Have you used one to say
"Thank you"?

—WILLIAM ARTHUR WARD

....

....

....

....

....

....

....

....

....

In ordinary life we hardly realize that we receive a great deal more than we give, and that it is only with gratitude that life becomes rich.

—Dietrich Bonhoeffer

....

....

....

....

....

....

....

....

....

We all live with the objective of being happy; our lives are all different and yet the same.

—ANNE FRANK

....

....

....

....

....

....

....

....

....

Let us rise up and be thankful, for if we didn't learn a lot today, at least we learned a little, and if we didn't learn a little, at least we didn't get sick, and if we got sick, at least we didn't die; so let us all be thankful.

—BUDDHA

Feeling grateful or appreciative of someone or something in your life actually attracts more of the things that you appreciate and value into your life.

—CHRISTIANE NORTHRUP

Gratitude Power Tools:

DON'T DAWDLE, DOODLE!

Use this page to harness the streams of your own consciousness. Doodle, draw, or write whatever comes to mind. Sit uninterrupted for a few minutes and what appears on the page might just open you up to explore and give thanks for that which lies beneath.

Sixty Seconds of Gratitude Practice

Margie Lapanja of Incline Village, Nevada, has this formula for tapping into gratefulness in our lives and making every day a thank-you.

She says, "Being grateful for the gifts you have been given, love being the most resplendent of all, is the very foundation of a timeless, joyous celebration of life. For the love you give *and* the love you receive to thrive with freshness, stability, and magic, always count and honor your blessings and gifts. A careless rain falls on the party whose revelers are numb with the side effects of living in a fast-forward world. If you don't make the effort to protect your love light with an umbrella of gratitude, your light will dim or be extinguished."

Here are some practices she suggests:

- Make a promise to yourself to consciously set aside a time each day (even if it is but 60 precious seconds) to fortify your belief in the miracle of love and keep the river of your soul flowing with clear and clean waters through the practice of gratitude.

- Upon waking, as you lie in bed drifting through your dreams, greet the glory of the new day with a sacred declaration of the power of love. Either aloud or in silence, recite this personal celebration of rebirth, new beginnings, and possibilities inspired by an Irish prayer, or create a canticle—and a time—of your own:

I arise this day
With love in my heart,
Through the warmth of the sun,
The radiance of the moon,
Freedom of the wind,
Joy of rushing water,
Splendor of fire,
Stability of earth,
Serenity of stars, and
the wisdom of silence.
I embrace this day
Through the grace of life to guide me
And the promise of love to inspire me.

Gratitude Questions:

WISDOM IS NOT THE "RIGHT ANSWERS," IT'S THE "RIGHT QUESTIONS"

1. *Who are the five most grateful people you know?*

....

....

....

....

....

2. *What makes them so content?*

....

....

....

....

....

....

....

3. *What can you learn from them?*

....

....

....

....

....

....

....

Now write a brief note to them thanking them for their attitudes of gratitude, saying that you truly appreciate who they are and that their sunny dispositions have affected you in a remarkable way.

....

....

....

....

....

....

Conclusion

OPENING A GRATITUDE CIRCLE

I n closing, we thought we would share with you one last way
that you can express all of this newfound gratitude, and that
is by opening up a "Gratitude Circle." The idea is simple. A gratitude circle is a place for sharing stories, photos, prayers of gratitude, and videos with friends and loved ones. The more people you
can get to align with you, the sooner you will discover the positive power of gratitude and reap the many benefits that come from
doing so.

We started our book and launched our Facebook "Living Life
as a Thank You" page with just the two of us—two moms who
lived across the country—Nina Lesowitz in the San Francisco Bay
Area and Mary Beth Sammons in the Chicago suburbs, in telephone

calls and e-mails sharing our gratefulness for the blessings that were pouring into our lives.

We started talking about how even in the most challenging of times—raising teens and facing financial uncertainty in the publishing profession where times have been tough—that even through this adversity, if we started our day with an attitude of gratitude, we could focus on what is possible in life and good things would come our way. Pretty soon, we had an entire community of friends, colleagues, and new people who found us through our book and on Facebook.

Now, we want to spread that gift and help you become cheerleaders for others who have tapped into the power of thankfulness by forming your own Gratitude Circle.

By creating a Gratitude Circle, you can join us in being grateful. Connect with others in this special group that's dedicated to honoring the simple phrases "Thank you" and "I am grateful for...." We know firsthand that once you start a thankfulness circle, it won't take long for others to join in, and the power of gratefulness will permeate and bless your everyday being.

There are several ways you can take part in a Gratitude Circle. You can set your intention to join a circle on our Facebook page, "Living Life as a Thank You," and immediately become part of our online community. Or you can create your own Gratitude Circle. We make it easy for you with our tips for starting a circle.

TIPS FOR GETTING STARTED

1. **Assume the role of Gratitude Guide.**

   As the organizer of the Gratitude Circle, consider yourself the host or hostess, almost as if you have invited a group of friends—or people you hope to become friends—to your dinner table. Your role is to help guide conversations and serve up a feast (of interesting stories about gratitude or nuggets of information to share) that will keep the conversations meaningful, inspiring, and ultimately bring to life the power of gratitude in all the lives of those gathered in your circle.

2. **Create a Mission or Goals for your Gratitude Circle.**

   What do you want to accomplish? How will you manifest gratitude in your own life and the lives of those in your circle? Will you share stories, inspiring quotes, guided meditations? Create a plan for guiding your group through the practice of gratitude.

3. **Decide whether to meet online or in person.**

   The exciting thing about the Internet is that you can create a Gratitude Circle and community online and connect friends and colleagues from across the country—and the world. See our Facebook page for inspiration. Or, you may want to create an in-person circle with friends in your neighborhood or town.

4. **Send out e-vites, invites, and make phone calls** to invite members to your Gratitude Circle. Ask everyone to invite a friend and spread the word about your new group.

5. **Select a meet-up place.** Often guides will invite in-person communities to meet at their home. Or you may opt for a local coffee shop or a comfortable meeting place where you can gather regularly.

6. **Create a calendar** of meet-up dates and distribute to your group.

7. **Create Gratitude Circle materials.** In our book, *Living Life as a Thank You,* we have lots of prompts for discussions about gratitude and thankfulness. Please feel free to tap into these as resources.

8. **Stay in touch with us.** We want to stay connected to YOU and help you spread the good news about what being thankful can do as it manifests in your life and the life of your friends, family, and members of your Gratitude Circle.

CIRCLES OF GRACE

Those simple suggestions should help you and your Gratitude Circle get started. Remember, nothing is cast in stone and you can feel free to improvise until you find your comfort zone. We guarantee you will come away from these gatherings feeling inspired, challenged, and with exciting new ideas to share.

First, begin by welcoming your guests. Go around the circle, each person introducing themselves. For example, "I am Mary Beth Sammons and I live in Chicago. I am a writer, literacy volunteer, and mother of two." Next read a passage of poetry, prayer, or prose. We recommend sections of either the introduction or the beginning of Chapter Two of this workbook. Now, go clockwise around the circle, and ask each participant why he or she is here and what spiritual sustenance he or she is seeking.

Ask a volunteer to read from the "Your Well-Being" section in Chapter One of the workbook. Lead the group in the "Gratitude Meditation: Love" you'll find there. You can continue on and do the gratitude exercise, if time permits. These group gatherings are wonderful, but personal sharing and goal discussion can be intimidating at first, so be mindful of your group and you'll sense when you need to wrap things up. Always end on a high note by asking each person to share a gratitude. May your transformation be your inspiration!

ABOUT THE AUTHORS

NINA LESOWITZ is a public relations practitioner and author who has been featured on national, state, and local television and radio as well as in newspaper and magazine articles. She served as a resident expert on PBS.org in 2010. Born in Brooklyn, New York, Nina has traveled extensively throughout the world and witnessed many acts of courageousness firsthand. She is the co-author of three bestselling books: *The Party Girl Cookbook* and, with Mary Beth Sammons, *Living Life as a Thank You* and *The Courage Companion*. Nina lives in Piedmont, California, with her husband, Martin, and two daughters.

MARY BETH SAMMONS is an award-winning journalist and author who writes about health, wellness, and reinventing your life in various print and online health and wellness sites such as AOL Health and the *Chicago Tribune*. She is a former bureau chief for Crain's Chicago Business and is the author of nine books, among them *Second Acts That Change Lives: Making a Difference in the World* and *My Family: Collected Memories*. She has received several industry awards, including first place from United Press International for best spot news coverage, a PR Silver Anvil Award, and an undergraduate scholarship from the William Randolph Hearst Foundation. She lives in the Chicago area with her three children.

90615